WHY

DO WE HAVE RULES IN SCHOOL?

THE COMMON GOOD

PATRICK HELY

PowerKiDS press.
New York

Published in 2019 by The Rosen Publishing Group, Inc.
29 East 21st Street, New York, NY 10010

First Edition

Editor: Jennifer Lombardo
Book Design: Tanya Dellaccio

Photo Credits: Cover Sergey Novikov/Shutterstock.com; p. 5 wavebreakmedia/Shutterstock.com; p. 7 gpointstudio/Shutterstock.com; p. 9 vgajic/E+/Getty Images; p. 11 RUSS ROHDE/Cultura/Getty Images; pp. 13, 19 Monkey Business Images/Shutterstock.com; p. 15 Lorena Fernandez/Shutterstock.com; p. 17 kali9/E+/Getty Images; p. 21 Syda Productions/Shutterstock.com; p. 22 ESB Professional/Shutterstock.com.

Cataloging-in-Publication Data

Names: Hely, Patrick.
Title: Why do we have rules in school? / Patrick Hely.
Description: New York : PowerKids Press, 2019. | Series: The common good | Includes glossary and index.
Identifiers: LCCN ISBN 9781538330920 (pbk.) | ISBN 9781538330913 (library bound) | ISBN 9781538330937 (6 pack)
Subjects: LCSH: Schools–Juvenile literature. | Student etiquette–Juvenile literature.
Classification: LCC BJ1857.S75 H45 2019 | DDC 395.5–dc23

Manufactured in the United States of America

CPSIA Compliance Information: Batch #CS18PK: For Further Information contact Rosen Publishing, New York, New York at 1-800-237-9932

Mar 19
J

CONTENTS

Your School Community

A community is a group of people who live or work in the same place and care about the same things. Community members often share similar values and ideas. People can belong to several communities, including their town and neighborhood. Your school is a type of community, too.

When people do things that **benefit** their whole community, they're working toward the common good. Working toward the common good keeps a community running smoothly. It also keeps community members happy. A simple way to contribute, or give, to the common good of your school community is by following the rules.

There to Learn

Think about a day at school. You likely have a lot of rules to follow. You might even think there are too many rules. Without rules, though, there would be chaos, or a total lack of order. Rules are important because they help everyone in your school community stay **focused** on learning.

By following rules, such as staying in your seat, you show respect for the other students in your classroom who are trying to learn. If you jumped out of your chair and ran around, you would be a distraction. Distractions are things that take attention away from something else, such as your teacher.

Schools have rules so there won't be problems inside or outside classrooms. When you follow the rules, it shows your teacher and classmates you care about your **education**. It also shows you care about your classmates' education. This makes **relationships** between you, your classmates, and your teacher better, which helps your school run better.

Fair and Safe

Schools have rules so every student has an equal chance to learn. Your teacher likely requires you to raise your hand before asking or answering questions. This is so everyone has a fair chance to speak. Rules against copying each other's homework or tests also keep learning fair for everyone.

Rules help make your school a safe place to learn, both inside and outside. Rules against running in the halls help students move around the school safely. Many students walk or ride their bikes to school. Rules about parking and when and where people can drive also help keep students safe.

Making the Rules

Principals and teachers make school rules. They work toward the common good of the school community by making rules they think are useful, fair, and good for everyone. If students follow the rules, it shows they're **responsible** and can be trusted. Sometimes students have the chance to help make their school's rules.

19

Your teachers and principal will notice and **appreciate** when you follow the rules. They'll also notice if you break a rule, and you'll get in trouble. For example, if you shout in class, you might have to miss recess. If your school has rules you don't understand, don't be afraid to ask an adult about them.

Reach Your Goals

Rules help a school community stay safe and focused on learning. When you follow the rules at school, it shows you respect your own education as well as the education of others. School rules help students reach their goals and be successful, which is good for everyone in the school community.

GLOSSARY

appreciate: To be thankful for someone or something.

benefit: To be helpful or useful to.

education: The act of learning or teaching.

focused: Giving directed attention to a task.

relationship: A connection between two or more people or things.

responsible: Showing care for things you have to do.

INDEX

WEBSITES

Due to the changing nature of Internet links, PowerKids Press has developed an online list of websites related to the subject of this book. This site is updated regularly. Please use this link to access the list: www.powerkidslinks.com/comg/school